WILMINGTON
through Italian eyes

WILMINGTON
through Italian eyes

Giuseppe D'Incà

Wilmington, Delaware

WILMINGTON
through Italian eyes

Published by: CEDAR TREE BOOKS, LTD.

First Edition

Any inquiries should be directed to:
Cedar Tree Books
9 Germay Drive
Wilmington, Delaware 19804
(302) 658-3994
books@ctpress.com
www.cedartreebooks.com

ISBN 1-892142-26-0

TITLE: Wilmington through Italian Eyes
PHOTOGRAPHY: Giuseppe D'Incà
TEXT: Constance J. Cooper - *The First City of the First State*
    Marjorie McNinch - *Saint Anthony's Italian Festival*
    Phil Maggitti - *A View from the Hill*
    Giuseppe D'Incà - *A New World City with Old World Roots*
EDITOR: Nicholas L. Cerchio III
COPY EDITOR: Phil Maggitti
BOOK DESIGN AND LAYOUT: Bob Schwartz

Library of Congress Cataloging-in-Publication Data

D'Incà, Giuseppe.
  Wilmington through Italian eyes / Giuseppe D'Incà.-- 1st ed.
    p. cm.
  Includes bibliographical references and index.
  ISBN 1-892142-26-0 (alk. paper)
 1. Italian Americans--Delaware--Wilmington--Social life and customs--Pictorial works. 2. Ethnic festivals--Delaware--Wilmington--Pictorial works. 3. Wilmington (Del.)--Social life and customs--Pictorial works. 4. Architecture--Delaware--Wilmington--Pictorial works. 5. Wilmington (Del.)--Buildings, structures, etc.--Pictorial works. 6. Wilmington (Del.)--Pictorial works. I. Title.

 F174.W743D56 2005
 975.1'200451'0222--dc22

2005006904

Printed and Bound on acid free paper by Grafica Piemontese, Volpiano, Turin, Italy

CONTENTS

ACKNOWLEDGMENTS

I would like to express my sincere gratitude to a number of people whose participation and assistance played an important part in the realization of this book:

Mary Ann Bogino, Ritchie De Vincentis, Adriano Ciancio (mayor of Olevano on the Tusciano), Alfonso Andria (member of the European Parliament), Pietro D'Aniello (president of the Olevano on the Tusciano Pro Loco - local cultural promotion office), Liliana Lepore, Filiberta Del Galdo, Pio Peruzzini, Egidio Bufano, Ralph Degli Obizzi, Bob Schwartz, Beverly and Nick Cerchio, Giuseppe Strafella, and all my friends on the Wilmington/Olevano and Olevano/Wilmington sister city committees.

Giuseppe D'Incà

INTRODUCTION

I would like to take this opportunity to express to the entire Olevano Pro Loco my extreme pleasure with this passionate, selfless work. I would also like to express my admiration for the sensibility and support of the local government of Olevano on the Tusciano.

Becoming a sister city to Wilmington, Delaware, in America is rife with meaning for the government as well as the citizens of Olevano on the Tusciano. Among the many benefits of this association, the recovery of an important part of the local identity of Olevano on the Tusciano is one of the most significant. The considerable number of citizens of Olevano in Wilmington has permitted, in fact, the rediscovery of origins, the re-establishment of affections, and the promotion of beneficial cultural exchanges. One of those exchanges, which occurred in June 2003, brought an official delegation from the Sister City of Wilmington to Olevano.

The rapport that has evolved between the two cities is further strengthened by Giuseppe D'Incà's valuable publication. Giuseppe has furnished, with his professional images, a representation of Wilmington as seen by Italian eyes through his camera lens.

The growth of our local communities depends on the vision and dedication of members who are firmly rooted in this area and who nurture its progress with their innovative, promotional resources. The strengthening of the idea of a united Europe in the collective conscience—especially following the expansion of the European Community—is a product of the initiatives and social-cultural dynamics of individual communities. Their resources are a shared richness that improves the lives of all their citizens.

Alfonso Andria
European Parliament Deputy

This photographic essay by Giuseppe D'Incà marks the first step of a journey taken by the cities of Wilmington, Delaware, and Olevano sul Tusciano, Italy, to create a sister city affiliation.

Two nations, two worlds, two different realities meet again after nearly a century to embrace one another and bring together many families that have been separated by distance and time.

The sister city relationship reinforces a bond that has linked the two communities for many years, if only as an abstraction. That bond is forged from the mutual rediscovery of common social and historic traditions, as well as feelings that originate from a deep and tangible link with a shared culture. It is a search for one's roots and one's past.

The photographic image serves in this context as a means of holding back time, capturing life's moments, and conveying its stories.

D'Incà's work brings Wilmington, with all its characteristics skillfully observed, to the people of Olevano sul Tusciano. Architecture and human figures that would normally pass unnoticed in the rush of daily life suddenly acquire new personality and new meaning. They are the unknown protagonists that become part of society, suddenly alive and fraught with emotion and sentiment.

In a captured gesture the hand of a subject seems to reach out from the page and invite the viewer to grasp it, to hold it tight. The image seems to seek our solidarity and intensity of feeling. It is the essence of life—a continuous succession of colorful events that would otherwise be replaced by others were it not for the photographic work that sets them on paper and fixes them indelibly in our minds.

Adriano Ciancio
Mayor, Olevano sul Tusciano

During the first years of the 20th Century, hundreds of citizens of Olevano Sul Tusciano bade farewell to family and friends before emigrating to the American city of Wilmington, Delaware. These emigrants intended to work long enough in America to improve their lot in life, then return to their homes in Italy.

The majority of these Olevanesi, however, did not return to Italy. Many of our parents, children, brothers and sisters, cousins and friends were never seen again. In the ensuing years the families on both sides of the ocean have grown. Several generations have passed, but the desire to reunite and rekindle past relationships has not. Time and distance could not annul the blood ties between people who lived for many years on different continents. The need to reestablish a connection has motivated our relatives and their descendents in Wilmington to rediscover their origins.

Through this book, Giuseppe D'Incà has brought the salient moments of this reunion between people who have grown up in two different, though almost complementary, worlds into sharp focus. In doing so he has created a work of art that will surely become a historical and artistic reference for future generations of these sister cities.

As photographed by D'Incà, the architecture of Wilmington appears as a logical continuation of the ancient and valuable monuments of Olevano Sul Tusciano. The two cities are united by the common origins and old traditions that the Olevanesi of Wilmington did not want to forget, and have kept alive in their minds, their hearts, and in their city.

Pietro D'Aniello
President, Olevano sul Tusciano Tourist Board
President, Picentia Tourism
Coordinator, Picentine Tourist Board

FOREWARD

The work presented on these pages was born of the desire of the "Olevanesi of Wilmington" to re-establish the ties that, until recently, had connected our respective communities.

In view of this desire, the Olevano on the Tusciano Pro Loco (local cultural promotion office) asked me, as a member and head of the photographic section, to participate in an ambitious project. The goal of the project was to rediscover—through an exploration of common experiences—the ties, beliefs, and sentiments that unite our communities.

Therefore, I decided to visit Wilmington during one of the most unifying moments any community experiences: a religious festival.

After arriving in Wilmington, I spent several days photographing the architectural and structural features of the city and its suburbs. Then I attended the Saint Anthony's Festival. This annual event, which is highly regarded throughout the greater Wilmington area, is well attended not only by members of Wilmington's Italian community but also by members of other ethnic groups.

Certainly a neighborhood festival is an ideal setting in which to capture the expressions, emotions, and spirit of a community. During a festival, particularly one dedicated to a saint, it is possible to grasp the soul of an occasion, the living moment, without the distorting filter of social conventions. During this neighborhood festival people gather to enjoy themselves and to celebrate lives lived far away in an Italy that also honors her saints with processions and gives homage to those heavenly beings who help and protect us.

I witnessed in Wilmington a strong, intense participation by her "Little Italy" community in the eucharistic celebration, the procession of the saint, who was, for this occasion, flanked by statues of other saints. Each devotee appeared engaged, sheltered, and protected by this historic, yet living, religious tradition.

Still, there was more—a hue, an originality, a folklore, new to my lens, born of America's melting-pot philosophy that brings diverse ethnicities, cultures, and traditions together. Seeing "panzarotti" side-by-side with steamy hotdogs gave me a feeling of comfort and repose. From that feeling grew hope and a certainty that it is possible, through individual and social enrichment, to share experiences that define different cultures.

Happily, we are now "sister cities". The rapport between us is no longer confined to correspondence between relatives. Instead the entire community of Olevano on the Tusciano has come to know its new, and at the same time old, friends in Wilmington.

Giuseppe D'Incà

WILMINGTON
through Italian eyes

WILMINGTON
the first city of the first state

Delaware's largest city, Wilmington is located on the Delaware River about 30 miles south of Philadelphia. A growing metropolis, Wilmington is surrounded by a large suburban area. According to the 2000 U.S. Government census, the city's population was 72,718.

In March 1638, European settlement began in the area that would become Wilmington. The first settlers were Swedish soldiers and farmers, who claimed the area as a colony of Sweden. Although New Sweden received little support from home, the farmers and soldiers kept the colony alive. It was conquered by the Dutch in 1655. Nine years later the English took control of the area, and it remained part of England's North American colonies until 1776.

From its beginning, the Wilmington area has been ethnically, racially, and religiously diverse. Swedish, Dutch, and English settlers lived on farms in the area for nearly a century, but there was no real town established until 1731, when Thomas Willing laid one out on the banks of the Christina River. He called it Willingtown, which was changed to Wilmington when the town received a royal charter in 1739.

Two smaller rivers flowing into the Delaware, the Christina and the Brandywine, provided a port for shipping and water power for manufacturing. Since the land surrounding Wilmington produced large crops of wheat and corn, successful flour mills developed along the Brandywine beginning in the early 1740s. Quakers provided economic and political leadership in early Wilmington.

By the 1770s, Wilmington had a population of about 1,200, making it the largest town in Delaware. During the American Revolution, British troops who had defeated George Washington's forces at the Battle of Brandywine in nearby Chadds Ford, Pennsylvania, occupied Wilmington between mid-September and mid-October 1777. The occupation was peaceful and the town was not harmed.

From its founding until the mid-1900s, Wilmington's growth and prosperity were based on manufacturing rather than trade or government. In the early 1800s, the flour mills gradually declined, but other industries took their place. Perhaps the most im-

portant was the gunpowder works established by E.I. du Pont in 1802. These would grow into a huge multinational chemical corporation during the 1900s.

Wilmington also produced ships, railroad cars, leather, textiles, and other products that were sold worldwide. Industrial employment attracted immigrants from many nations, including Italians in the late 1800s and early 1900s. Wilmington grew rapidly from 8,452 people in 1840 to a peak population of 112,504 in 1940. The city was Delaware's center for shopping and entertainment as well as business and industry.

The immense needs of World War II provided a final burst of industrial prosperity, but since then Wilmington has changed greatly. Manufacturing has declined while the headquarters and research facilities of DuPont and other chemical companies have attracted executives and professionals to the area. New laws passed in the 1980s attracted credit card-issuing banks to Wilmington and its suburbs.

Today, most immigrants come from Asia, Mexico, and Latin America. Suburban residential, entertainment, and shopping areas have grown tremendously while the city itself has lost population, as is the case in many American cities. Revitalization programs are bringing new housing, shopping, and entertainment to the city, promising to restore energy and vibrancy to Wilmington.

Constance J. Cooper

WILMINGTON
a view from the hill

The notion of an Italian enclave in Wilmington, a clearly defined, homogeneous Little Italy that resonates exclusively to Italian cultural themes, is a romantic concept more than a physical reality. Yet what an interesting concept it is.

Wilmington's Little Italy—whose residents are wont to call The Hill—is a 70-square-block area in the southwest section of the city bounded by Eleventh Street on the north, Lancaster Avenue on the south, Broom Street on the east, and Union Street on the west. Even though it is not an ethnic monolith, it is home to enough Italian businesses and individuals to be infused with a subtle but distinct Mediterranean flavor.

The principal landmark on The Hill is St. Anthony of Padua church, a magisterial presence whose construction in the mid-1920s was accomplished under the occasionally gruff, always confident hand of John Francis Tucker, OSFS, an Irish priest born in Wilmington and educated in Rome.

Father Tucker's visibility on The Hill, where he presided as pastor of St. Anthony's from 1924 until 1949, should serve as a reminder that The Hill was never exclusively Italian. Living among the Di Sabatinos, Del Campos, Rovittis, Petrillos, and Fidanzas who settled this area, were O'Malleys, Pierkowskis, and Joneses too.

A few Italian immigrants had arrived on The Hill by the early 1880s. They came to work on the Baltimore and Ohio Railroad, located not far to the west of Union Street. One of those workers, Nicola Fidanza, came to Wilmington by way of Schenectady, New York, whence he had immigrated in 1879 as a twenty-three-year-old recently married man. After working four years as a carpenter in Schenectady, he moved to Wilmington to become the construction foreman on the B & O Railroad.

Fidanza opened The Hill's first Italian bakery and its first Italian steamship agency. After building a large house for himself on Scott Street in 1888, he became active in the construction business. Before he died in 1929, he had built upwards of 250 and perhaps as many as 500 houses in Wilmington. Fidanza purchased lots from people with old Wilmington family names such as Bush, Hilles, Field, Chandler, Gregg, and Tatnall, then built houses on those lots and sold the houses to Italians. He was arguably the most influential person in the establishment and growth of The Hill.

By 1900, the Italian population of Delaware was 1,122, nearly three times what it had been a decade earlier. That population would double during the next two decades, reaching 3,000 in 1930, where it remained until 1960. Most Italians arriving in Wilmington settled near the undeveloped western edge of the city.

Before 1900 there was little sense of community among Italians in Wilmington. They had come from many towns and villages in Italy, therefore, differences in dialects hindered communication somewhat. There were no mutual-aid societies at the time, nor did the church serve as a rallying point for immigrants. The family was paramount, and a majority of the Italians who settled in Delaware soon had wives and children.

The majority of the Italian-born adult population of Wilmington comprised first-generation immigrants until well into the second decade of the twentieth century. By the time the second generation— the children born in America— reached maturity, their parents had gradually incorporated American values and ideals into their way of life. They lived in American style houses and sent their children to American schools, yet they tended to speak Italian at home and were adamant about following an Italian diet, which did not include large amounts of meat and fat.

By 1910, close to half the Italian heads of households in Wilmington had become citizens. They

could speak English and could also read and write. There were, however, many Italian-American heads of households who could read and write Italian, but not English.

About one-sixth of the Italian immigrants who lived in Delaware in 1910 owned their own houses. By then a number of Italians had left the laboring trades to start their own shoemaker's shops, barbershops, grocery stores, saloons, bakeries, tailor shops, and restaurants.

The Hill was Wilmington's acknowledged Little Italy by the time construction began on St. Anthony's church. Other pockets of Italian settlement existed then—The Valley (bounded by Front Street on the south, Ninth Street on the north, West Street on the west, and Monroe street on the east); the East Side (bounded by Second Street on the south, Sixth Street on the North, Poplar Street on the east, and Market Street on the West); and the Eleventh Street Bridge area (whose boundaries were Vandever Avenue, the Brandywine River, Market Street, and Claymont Street).

Whatever distinctly Italian character existed in those colonies was eventually absorbed in the name of progress. Today only The Hill, with its magnificent church and its wildly popular annual festival, serves as a testimony to the contributions made to the city of Wilmington by her Italian sons and daughters.

Phil Maggitti

WILMINGTON

saint anthony's italian festival

Each June, St. Anthony's Italian Festival brings eight days of entertainment, music, amusements, food, and drink to the vicinity of St. Anthony of Padua Church. Hundreds of thousands of people from the Wilmington area, neighboring states, and Italy itself attend the festival. In short the festival is big business.

Running annually since 1975, the festival has its roots in the Italian immigrant settlement known as "Little Italy." It takes its name from Little Italy's parish church, St. Anthony of Padua, built in 1926.

During the 1880s, Italians coming to Wilmington formed their own Italian enclave in an area called The Hill, today's Little Italy. As the population increased, social institutions were established and religious practices maintained to aid these Italian Americans in coping with their new surroundings and language. By 1920, the Italian American community on The Hill was large enough to merit a parish church. John Francis Tucker, OSFS, who was fluent in Italian, was appointed to the parish, called St. Anthony's, in 1924.

Following its completion, St. Anthony's church was dedicated on June 13, 1926, the Feast Day of St. Anthony. The dedication and following celebration drew 3,000 inside and 2,000 outside the church.

With the new church came religious festivals, an important part of life in this Italian colony. By 1936, there were at least three prominent annual festivals at St. Anthony's: the Feast of St. Anthony, the Feast of St. Rocco, and the Feast of Our Lady of Mt. Carmel. Because these festivities took so much planning and involved so much of church officials' time, those involved in presenting the festivals decided to have one festival instead of three.

St. Anthony's Festival still offers Italian music and song as well as Italian dishes and wine. The Festival had grown so in attendance (350,000 in 1996), that more dining space is used, and a shuttle service alleviates some of the parking nightmares. Planning for each new festival begins as soon as the current festival ends.

Festival entertainment has expanded to include bands and musical groups playing modern music, and a midway with a high-wire act. Before 1936, houses along the bor-

dering streets were decorated in multicolored lights and American as well as Italian flags. With the growth of the festival, more attention is paid today to saving parking in front of one's house than to its decoration.

The rich heritage of the festival, however, is preserved in the celebration of the Feast Days of the Saints. To honor twelve special saints, there is a procession in the afternoon of the second Sunday, the last day, of the festival. The statues of the twelve saints are drawn on wheeled platforms through the streets around the church. On June 13 a special mass is said for St. Anthony on his feast day.

During the eight-day festival, more than 40,000 spaghetti and ravioli dinners are served in two dining rooms. Half a dozen or more outdoor eating places and cafes provide different fare. A variety of national musical entertainment occurs nightly. Once all of the bills for putting on this festival are paid, St. Anthony's nets somewhere around $300,000.

Marjorie G. McNinch

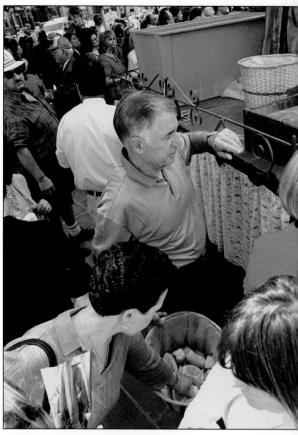

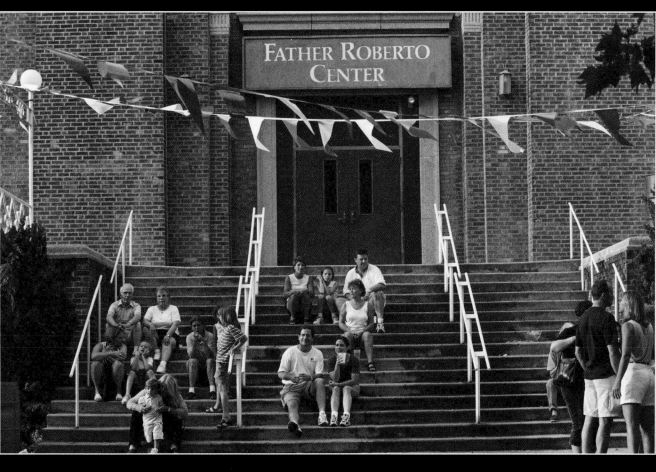

WAGER 25¢ TO $1.00
IF YOU DON'T UNDERSTAND THE GAME,
ASK THE CLERK
THEN IF YOU STILL DON'T UNDERSTAND,
DON'T PLAY
No Tipping

CLARENCE J. VENE
COMPLETE BINGO SUPPLIES   FOLDING TABLES AND
LEVITTOWN, PA.   PHONE: 215-547-

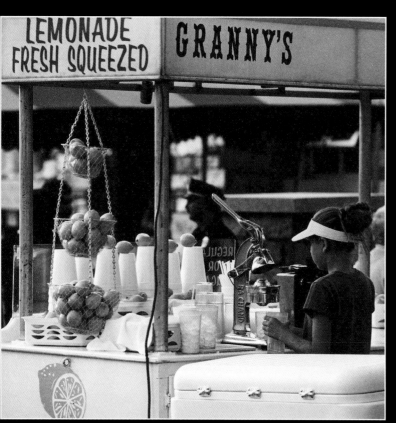

SUFFER THE LITTLE CHILDREN
TO COME UNTO ME

Detail of one of the Byzantine frescoes (*Traditio legis et clavium*) in the Grotto of Saint Michael at Olevano sul Tusciano.

WILMINGTON

a new world city with old world roots

Throughout written history the region of Italy nurtured by the Tusciano river has been inhabited, first by the Etruscans, then the Greeks and Romans who gave the river, which marks their southern-most expansion in Italy, its name. Known today as Olevano sul Tusciano, this area, which is located a short distance inland from the Tyrrhenian seacoast, is the gateway to the Regional Park of Monti Picentini and is Wilmington's sister city in Italy.

For centuries Olevano sul Tusciano was an ecclesiastical fiefdom governed by the Archbishopric of Salerno. Today the picturesque region is home to a confederation of three small towns—Salitto, Ariano, and Monticelli—and a population of 70,000. This charming area owes its name to the extensive cultivation of olives begun there by Greek settlers.

Foremost among the many significant cultural sites in Olevano sul Tusciano is the Grotto of Saint Michael, which is one of only a hundred sites in the world included on the World Monument Fund of New York's preservation list. The grotto is also a candidate to become one of UNESCO's World Heritage sites.

Inside the grounds of the grotto are several funeral chapels (Martyria) and a tri-lobed basilica with Byzantine frescoed walls, whose remarkable workmanship is attributed to a community of Byzantine monks that once lived there.

These monks were eventually replaced by Benedictine monks. During the Christological cycle of the frescos, they introduced images related to the cult of Saint Peter. A tunnel connecting the Grotto of Saint Michael to the Grotto of Nardantuono commands the interest of scholars because of the Bronze Age artifacts it contains.

Along the road approaching the Grotto of Saint Michael are the ruins of the Cella of Saint Vincent, a small convent of historical significance. The *Cronicon Volturense* of Monk John describe a certificate issued in Aquisgrana on January 11, 819, by the emperor Ludivico, who donated to the monastery of Saint Vincent at Volturno properties that included the Cella of Saint Vincent at Tusciano.

To safeguard the sacred hermitage, the impenetrable and well-rooted Castrum Olibani,

103

a Longobard castle, was built between two rocky masses on the bordering hill. Although the castle is in ruins today, enough of its magnificence remains to give a clear idea of what the original structure was like.

At the foot of the castle, the Dominican convent built in 1533 also lies in ruins. Nevertheless, the scope of its outstanding architecture can still be imagined.

Near the base of the hill sits the Longobard Curtis of Santa Maria. A site of archeological and architectural interest, the Longobard Curtis is a unique example of a ninth century "curtis," a Longobard term used during the Middle Ages to indicate autonomous farm areas. Because this site was built on a pre-existing Roman struc-

ture, is also known as the "Roman villa."

Separating the Castrum Olibani from the Grotto of Saint Michael is the Tusciano River, which still conserves corners of uncontaminated beauty. Its crystalline waters are home to an authochonal species of flavorful trout, the "fario."

The three communities nestled in Olevano sul Tusciano—along with the churches and buildings there—make up the cultural mosaic of the region. By reason of the great tourist potential contained in this mosaic, Olevano sul Tusciano is a vital element in the development of the entire area and of the tourist system of Monti Picentini.

Olevano sul Tusciano is in fact a confederation of three small towns: Ariano (top left), Salitto (bottom left), and Monticelli (below).

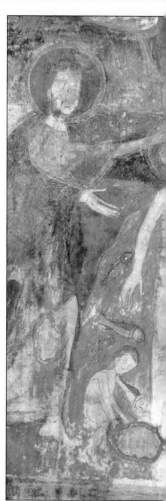

The Madonna Hodighitria chapel on the grounds of the Grotto of Saint Michael (upper left).

Funeral chapels (martyria) in the Grotto of Saint Michael (upper center).

Dominican convent (top).

Portico of the Dominican Convent (above).

Details of some of the Byzantine frescoes in the Grotto of Saint Michael at Olevano sul Tusciano: crucifixion of Christ (left center), baptism of Jesus (center), Traditio legis et clavium - Jesus gives the keys to Saint Peter and the laws to Saint Paul (lower left) and Jesus being presented at the temple (center left).

A 16th century frescoe of Saint James adorns the walls of the Dominican convent (left).

Detail of the entrance to the Castrum Olibani, a Longobard castle built for defensive purposes on the hills above Olevano sul Tusciano (upper left).

Guard tower and living quarters of the Castrum Olibani (lower left).

Monte Raione as seen from the Castrum Olibani (center).

Olevano sul Tusciano owes the first part of its name to the extensive cultivation of olives begun there by Greek settlers (left and below) and the second part to the river (bottom) that winds along the valley floor.

Procession of Saint Michael (upper left, above and left).

Antique mill from 1700 (far left).

A view of the town of Ariano (center left).

Arrivederci

Giuseppe D'Incà